OUTRAGEOUS LEARNING
AN EDUCATION MANIFESTO

OUTRAGEOUS
LEARNING

AN
EDUCATION
MANIFESTO

BY
SCOTT D. OKI

FOUNDATIONAL THOUGHTS ON REFORMING
OUR PUBLIC SCHOOLS

POLICY CENTER

A publication of the Washington Policy Center

Inquiries and book orders should be addressed to:
P.O. Box 3643 Seattle, WA 98124-3643
Phone: 206 937 9691   Fax: 206 624 8038

www.outrageouslearning.org

Washington Policy Center is an independent, nonprofit 501(c)(3)
research and education organization.

ISBN 978-0-9765758-1-8

DEDICATION

TO MY GRANDPARENTS,
KITARO & SHIZUNO OKI,
AND JUKICHI & KIYO HAMASAKI,
FOR THE COURAGE TO EMIGRATE
FROM JAPAN AND
FOR MAINTAINING THEIR HONOR
THROUGH TRYING TIMES

TO MY PARENTS,
KIYOTO & KIMIKO OKI,
FOR SACRIFICING SO MUCH SO THEIR KIDS
COULD HAVE A CHANCE TO SUCCEED

TO LAURIE,
AND THE FUTURE OF ALL CHILDREN,
INCLUDING OUR OWN,
ALEXANDER, NICHOLAS, AND CALLAN

FOREWORD

DANIEL MEAD SMITH
PRESIDENT, WASHINGTON POLICY CENTER

We are pleased to publish this new book by Scott Oki describing his ideas for improving our public education system, and how schools can deliver "outrageous learning" to all students. Washington Policy Center feels this book is a unique opportunity to spread Scott's hopeful message that improving the education of all children is possible. After all, our mission is to improve the lives of citizens through better public policy, and that is what this book is all about.

Washington Policy Center is a non-profit, non-partisan research organization in Seattle, Washington. We are a "think tank," not a trade association or lobbying organization. We testify before legislative committees when invited and work with policymakers at their request. We do, however, measure the impact of our ideas. It is one thing to publish studies and hold events, and another to have our ideas and analyses influence the public debate. That is the basis for this book. We are confident Scott's book will influence the debate surrounding education reform, and better still, that policymakers will recognize the wisdom that lies behind his recommendations.

Our nation's education system continues to fall behind the rest of the world. Two recent government reports reveal that public education officials are producing a generation of students less educated than their parents.

We can improve the education we provide our children. Scott offers concrete policy recommendations to do just that, and to ensure that the next generation of students receive the best education possible.

None of us can reform education by ourselves. Policymakers, parents, school board members, superintendents, principals and teachers must become involved if we are to improve our schools. There is nothing more important than preparing our young people for a fulfilling and prosperous future.

I encourage you to contact us at 206 937 9691, wpc@washingtonpolicy.org, and to visit our special website for this book project, www.outrageouslearning.org with your comments, or to order additional copies of this book, or any of our individual studies on education reform.

On behalf of our board of directors, advisory board members and staff, thank you for your interest in this book and in our work to improve the lives of current and future generations.

CONTENTS

MEA CULPA

"When you come to a fork in the road, take it."
YOGI BERRA

About a year ago, I was facing a harsh reality and something about which I had been in deep denial...my 60th birthday would soon be upon me. Since retiring from Microsoft 17 years ago, I have been a full-time volunteer in the non-profit sector, dutifully and most-of-the-time joyfully pursuing my personal mission statement: "To marry my passion for things entrepreneurial and things philanthropic in ways that encourage others to do the same."

My wife Laurie and I founded The Oki Foundation in 1987. The beneficiaries of our foundation are largely non-profit charities focused on children's health and welfare issues. We intentionally excluded giving to public school education reform, because we did not think we could move the needle, that is, make a difference, in any significant way. So what changed our minds?

My first attempt at "retirement" resulted in a full-time, unpaid position as Chief Volunteer for The Oki Foundation. After 16 years of active volunteerism and at 60 years of age, I felt I had earned the right to really retire, to lay back, plop my feet on the table, smell the roses, pursue a few long-overdue hobbies, and do what I do best...sleep.

So I mentioned to Laurie that I planned to resign from most of the 26 non-profit boards on which I served. I would still be actively engaged in a handful of charities, but nothing close to my past commitment. Laurie asked, "What are you going to do with your new-found time?" I think she was a bit worried I would spend more time than she preferred at home. It was Laurie who suggested I find something that would fill up my idle bandwidth. I asked, "And what would that be?" She suggested that I try to make a difference with public school reform.

What were her reasons for choosing such an ambitious goal for me? I have always liked big challenges. I am good at thinking outside the box. And, perhaps most importantly, there really is nothing more important to the future of our country than to make sure all children have the foundational tool they need to prosper...an education. And so the journey begins.

It has been said that philosophers know a great deal about general theory and very little about specific details. And it has been said of experts that they know a great deal about details, but cannot see broad themes. I am neither a philosopher nor an expert. The result? I know too little about everything! But that doesn't stop me from having an opinion on this subject.

These thoughts and ruminations are offered from the perspective of someone who received his education, at elementary school, middle school, high school, college and graduate school, from the public system. My children, however, have never attended a public school. They are educational works-in-progress of some of the finest independent private schools in the country.

As a parent, I am guilty of taking the easy path and sending my children to private schools. But my wife and I did not want to risk our children's futures on the uncertainties and inadequacies of the public school system. Sadly, we felt that private schools were the best option. They have smaller class sizes, uniforms, discipline, nurturing, technology, safe learning environments, and an engaged school community. This is a conclusion, I might add, that we share with many public school administrators and teachers, and many politicians, who send their children to private schools.

It is my sincere hope that the thoughts that follow will at a minimum cause you either to vigorously agree or strongly disagree, or some combination of the two, but apathy is simply not acceptable. I hope you will engage your family and friends in a spirited discussion about one or more of the reform planks I present here. Invite your neighbor for a double-tall, non-fat, extra hot, half vanilla, triple shot latté and debate the issues. Get your book club involved. In the best of circumstances, maybe it will spur you to be an agent for change.

Whether you agree or disagree with me about the ideas presented in this book, change of some kind is sorely needed to reform our public school system. Change can only start when enough of us take the first step of communicating our views in a way that cannot be ignored. Like a little snowball that starts rolling down the slope, picking up speed, weight and size, by vocalizing our concerns we can perhaps create an avalanche that will shake the current system to its core. Our kids deserve no less.

PREFACE

"The sky is falling! The sky is falling!"
CHICKEN LITTLE

A re we being hysterical about the state of public education today? Hardly. Is the educational decline of the United States rooted to the ongoing failure of our K-12 public school system? Absolutely. Is the danger imminent? Yes. Do we really need to change the perception of public education of the past few generations? There is no question in my mind that vast, comprehensive change is necessary.

We lament the downward path of our K-12 public school education system. The United States spends $500 billion a year just maintaining the public school systems we have now. We devote billions more public and private dollars each year to try to improve and fix them. With great fanfare Congress passed federal education legislation, the No Child Left Behind Act, which too few people believe is making any difference and too many people feel is more of a hindrance than a help. There are too many indicators that we are on a negative spiral; and, as the concentric circles tighten, we accelerate down the path toward mediocrity...or worse.

So, where is the public outrage? I believe the lack of sufficient emotional energy to make a positive difference in public education is due to the fact that we, as individuals, feel powerless to fix a problem that is a multi-headed hydra of gargantuan size. Sure, individual schools may benefit from intense, critical intervention that turns them into great schools. But these are isolated cases. There are no examples of failing school *systems* that have been fixed.

Parents have little individual power to make any sense out of where to attack the problem. Those parents who have the economic means simply vote with their feet, and their bank accounts, and enroll their children in the best private schools. Parents who are not this fortunate are in a sense victims of the public monopoly. They resign themselves to trying to make the best out of the system they are given, or worse, they simply give up.

American employers, however, do not have the option of just giving up. In a modern economy, business owners need a well-educated work force, so improving schools is in their enlightened self-interest. Yet, there is no concerted effort from leaders in corporate America to force systemic change. The largest consumers of intellectual capacity (bio-technology, information technology, aerospace and other hard science-based companies) can afford to hire the best and the brightest from America's and other nations' institutions of higher learning. The United States imports 107,000 H-1B visa professionals every year; half of them have doctoral degrees. The largest companies do not necessarily feel the pain of low-performing public schools or of hiring inadequately trained employees.

Too often, owners of medium and small businesses are forced to compete for the best human capital against their much larger, and usually better financed, brethren. Many businesses are focused on short-term profitability at the expense of under-investing in education infrastructure change. The urgency to meet quarterly profit goals trumps spending money over 100 fiscal quarters on something as ethereal as "improving public education."

Perhaps the most leverage is wielded by those in government. Yet politicians cannot seem to muster the will to pass legislation that would truly reform the public school system. They do not want to raise taxes to fund reform, are unwilling to prioritize public school reform ahead of other pressing budget needs, and are afraid to confront powerful special interest groups. Of course, this sets the wrong tone and mindset. We really need to ask special interest groups, like the teachers' unions, to become advocates for change so they are no longer viewed as the primary obstacle to education reform.

Defining the Problem

So, what *is* the problem in public education?

Clearly, there are many indications that our public school system is ailing. The Bill and Melinda Gates Foundation Annual Report states:

> "Our education system is not preparing our young people for success. This year, more than 1 million students will drop out of high school." [Bill & Melinda Gates Foundation Report, 2008, page 13.]

The Children's Defense Fund estimates that one high school student drops out every nine seconds. For those kids who do not drop out, the picture is far from rosy.

Math and science test scores offer the only common basis for comparing U.S. schools to the rest of the world. By grade four, American students only score in the middle of 26 countries reported in the Third International Mathematics and Science Study (TIMSS). By grade eight, they are in the bottom third. By high school, they are near dead last.

The results of the 2007 Washington State Assessment of Student Learning (WASL) showed fewer than 60 percent of students met the math requirement. Forty-nine percent of sophomore high school students failed the WASL math test in 2007. This result was so alarming the legislature cancelled the math and science requirements in the WASL for graduation from high school for five years. But it gets more troubling.

Of the kids who do pass the WASL and go on to college, too many of them must take remedial courses in math to learn what they should have learned in high school. There are so many college freshmen who can't do basic math that some teachers at the University of Washington dumb down their class content to accommodate them. In fact, 60 U.W. professors signed an open letter in this regard.

According to Partnership For Learning, nearly 50 percent of recent high school graduates going to community college take remedial, pre-college math classes before they can begin credit-bearing work. Remediation is especially pronounced for minority students. Sixty-five percent of Latino students and 59 percent of African American students must take remedial classes in college.

There are other symptoms of systemic failure in public education. For the first time in U.S. history, the current generation is less educated than their parents. In the final 2006 report of *Washington Learns, World Class, Learner-Focused, Seamless Education*, chaired by Governor Christine Gregoire, "Younger adults in our state have, on average, less education than boomers." Nationally, based on SAT scores, the quality of students

applying to schools of education, those training to become
teachers, come from the lowest tier of college applicants.
[http://nces.ed.gov/programs/digest/d06/tables/dt06_133.asp.]

Research by the University of Washington College of Education
found that student performance improves when the diversity
of the teaching force matches the diversity of the student body.
Yet, the racial and ethnic diversity of teachers (seven percent) is
significantly lower than the diversity of students as a whole
(30 percent).

It is easy to be blinded and disillusioned by all of the bad news.
But the real problem, and the eventual cure, is rooted in just a
few essential things. First, there is an almost total lack of freedom for school leaders—principals and superintendents—
to innovate, make policy corrections and change any number
of things when warranted. Second, there are an insufficient
number of capable, insanely great teachers in the classroom,
and there are many weak teachers who should receive heavier
and more frequent doses of professional development, or who
should seek another line of work. And third, in many places,
there is a lack of involvement of parents and neighborhood
communities in improving local schools.

I strongly believe that the main reason we have been unable to
fix the public school system is *there is not a unified view of what*

the problem really is. Without a common, holistic view of the central problem, it is impossible to attack it in a coordinated fashion. The cure will elude us as we continue to throw nice-sounding palliatives at something that requires far more substantive remedies. We will remain detached, indifferent and ineffectual. Even with a common view, it will be extraordinarily difficult to fix a problem that is so immense, cumbrous and chronic.

Open and honest communication is essential to accomplishing most anything. I have held and applied this long-standing belief throughout my career. Being able to have a reasonable discussion about a serious problem, without some hidden agenda, leads to better outcomes and real solutions. It is absolutely essential to do so when trying to fix the largest, most entrenched problems imaginable, like improving the public education system. We might not like what we have to say to each other, but if we can have lively, even raucous debate on the issues, we will all be better for it.

OUTRAGEOUS LEARNING
AN EDUCATION MANIFESTO

"All who have meditated on the art of governing mankind have been convinced that the fate of empires depends on the education of youth."

ARISTOTLE, ON EDUCATION

The purpose of this book is to provide a framework for effecting positive, systemic improvement in our public school system. To gain real and lasting improvement, we must create positive change in virtually all areas of public education.

Only a long-term commitment to top-to-bottom reform will help. Nothing short of a willingness to think broadly and creatively will offset the massive inertia that stifles any hope of changing our public school system on a large-scale basis. Nothing short of a thorough, common sense and mutually-supporting plan will work.

We stand at a perilous point. If we do not fix our K-12 public school system soon, we risk becoming a second-class nation. We face the growing problem of our nation's youth not receiving an education that will secure their future and lead to enhanced economic growth. More of our young people should graduate from high school with the requisite skills that get them into college or on a vocational track, which in turn will lead to personal fulfillment and to productive citizenship.

Two key facts highlight the inadequacies of our public schools. First, in the U.S., every nine seconds a student drops out of high school. That is 2,500 students each day; over one million a year. Second, 68 percent of prison inmates are dropouts. The two facts are related. Once young people drop out of school, their chances of running afoul of the law increases greatly. Also, U.S. Census Bureau data shows students who drop out are much more likely to live in poverty than their peers who remain in school.

What is the ultimate goal of public education? It may seem admirable to prepare all kids for college, but not all kids may want to go to college. Public schools should prepare students to be appropriately trained for college, work and/or citizenship. As a society, we need to be more sensitive to the goals and passions of high school students, and allow them to pursue alternative education tracks, not just college. In education, one size does not fit all.

For example, it makes no sense to prepare students for college by requiring them to take three years of math when college entrance generally requires four years of math. It makes little sense to require all students to take three years of foreign language classes, when some of them may be headed to a vocational school to become auto technicians.

THE ELEVEN PLANKS OF
OUTRAGEOUS LEARNING

The following eleven ideas capture the main areas of focus for systemic public school reform. Although each area is substantial in itself, we must resist focusing on one proposal at the expense of the others. These ideas are all critical elements of a single, overall plan of improvement.

I

PLANK ONE:
LET LOCAL LEADERS LEAD

"Governing a great nation is a lot like cooking a fish –
too much handling will spoil it."
LAO TSU
CHINESE TAOIST PHILOSOPHER, FOUNDER OF TAOISM

What is the best way to organize public education governance and leadership? We no longer live in an age when the local one-room schoolhouse defines how children receive their education. Today, public education is decidedly centralized and involves strict controls not only at the district level, but at the state and federal level as well. The smothering effect of top-down controls raises a vital question, "Might we not be better off with a return to more local education governance?"

All organizations have one thing in common. They are run, whether effectively or ineffectively, by human beings. There are many types of organizations, with different leadership styles, various management practices, vertical, horizontal, circular, and even upside-down structures. Ultimately, however, all effective organizations must start with inspired leaders who are empowered to make key decisions and who accept responsibility for delivering results. The same principle applies to public schools.

The role of teachers

The classroom is the primary venue where the transfer of knowledge from the teacher to the student actually takes place. In order to maximize this knowledge transfer, I think teachers need to feel that they own what happens in their classroom. Teachers should be able to make the decisions that impact the learning for each and every one of their students without the burdensome constraints of bureaucracy. Periodically, even the very best teachers will require support.

This support usually comes from other teachers and the principal of the school. But teachers should also be able to rely on parent volunteers, student mentors, peer tutors, and the increased bandwidth and helping hands of the to-be-formed Teach Corps (see Plank Six). As leaders in the classroom, teachers need to be held accountable for the educational outcomes of their students.

Teachers, and students, are entitled to a safe, well-managed and caring learning environment. Teachers should have a say in which students remain in their classroom. They should also have a say in what discipline policies they need to maintain order, and when misbehaving students should be removed, so that cooperative students are not cheated of the opportunity to learn.

The role of principals

The position of principal is the most important leadership role in the management of a school. Principals should assume the role of CEO of their schools, with the ability to exercise leadership in seven key areas:

1. Establish and preserve a culture of excellence;
2. Carry out the strategic plans and policies that the Board of Directors approve (discussed below);
3. Keep the Board of Directors informed on key factors affecting the school community and support and be responsive to the ad hoc information needs of the Board of Directors;
4. Manage and inspire the members of his team;
5. Oversee the design and delivery of quality education programs;
6. Ensure the financial stability of the school, and;
7. Communicate openly and honestly with parents, teachers, students and the public.

Principals should be more than just building managers. The prerequisites for being a school principal should entail more than a three year tenure as a teacher.

The skill set required for a principal is very different than the skill set for a teacher. As the school's Chief Executive Officer, the principal should be ultimately responsible for the quality of the teachers, the effectiveness of the instruction and the health of the school's learning community (teachers, students, parents, mentors, tutors, physical plant, etc).

Principals should be dispensers of tough love. If a child is failing, teachers need to alert the parents and initiate remedial action at the earliest possible time. The principal should be the first line of support for the teachers. Both the teacher and the principal should be held accountable when they fail to intervene in time to save a child's education.

The principal should be central to the leadership in the school community. They should be inspiring, entrepreneurial, willing to make the tough decisions, fiscally responsible, and above all, they must demand excellence. Principals should provide critical leadership that inspires creativity and a can-do, positive attitude in the school. District officials and state legislators should release principals from bureaucratic shackles and let them become real leaders in the community.

The current mindset for many school district administrators is to expect the principal to do all of the above...but they are unwilling to delegate the authority or the resources for principals to really make a difference. Too many decisions are made centrally. There are too many constraints imposed by collective bargaining agreements to make mid-course corrections. Too little discretion is given to principals to hire and fire, or to inspire and develop their education teams. There are too many districts that impose standardized curriculum decisions. Principals can, of course, fail in one or more critical areas of leadership. But, if they are never even allowed the necessary freedom and resources to lead, we will never know how great, great can be.

Support for principals – the local Board of Directors

Principals, like all of us, need help to succeed. There are too few professional training opportunities specifically tailored to developing effective principals. Similar to the way a Board of Directors guides and supports the Chief Executive Officer of a for-profit company, school principals should be supported by a volunteer board of five to nine community-minded citizens, such as parents, business executives or retirees.

These boards are essential to running private, independent schools, but they are curiously absent from the public system. It would be the board's responsibility to hire and fire the principal, and to hold the principal accountable for achieving learning outcomes. It would also be the board's role to help the principal run his "business," that is, responsibly manage, operate, and conduct the affairs of a school that provides an excellent education for students.

Filling the position for Board of Directors for a local public school should be by gubernatorial appointment or by a surrogate appointed by the governor. While there is no guarantee that an appointed board would function any better than an elected board, I feel there are some significant advantages. First, an appointed system will result in better qualified candidates, if only because many qualified candidates have no desire to run a political campaign for such a position. Second, because of the sheer number of positions that need to be filled, an elective scenario is probably not practical. There are 2,318 public schools in Washington state multiplied by seven board seats, equals 16,226 positions to be filled. And third, appointed boards should be more objective in their decision making since they would be less beholden to political influences.

Just as individual schools should have an appointed board, school districts should also have appointed boards. These school district boards would work with their district superintendent.

Finally, all of the district superintendents should report to a cabinet-level, governor-appointed Secretary of Education.

II

PLANK TWO:
INSANELY GREAT TEACHERS

*"Look, I don't really know where we should take this bus.
But, I know this much: If we get the right people on the bus,
the right people to the right seats, and the wrong people off the bus,
then we'll figure out how to take it someplace great."*
FROM JIM COLLINS' #1 BESTSELLER, *GOOD TO GREAT*

Teachers have enormous influence on how well students
learn. Great teachers produce better student learning
than not-so-great teachers. In fact, dedicated teachers always
find a way to teach, even in the face of enormous obstacles,
like high student-to-teacher ratios, lack of supplies, and inferior
or inadequate classrooms. We should create a meritocracy in
which good teachers are recognized and paid for superior
teaching performance.

We should let schools take full advantage of the current insanely
great teachers by allowing them to work as "Master Teachers"
who help their colleagues become better teachers. Master
Teachers would be mentors to others in the profession, offering assistance in class or in training seminars. Master Teachers

could also be part of a peer review process that identifies and fosters rising talent within the teaching profession.

We should create a more exciting career path for teachers that provides opportunities for teachers to earn higher pay based on performance, rather than simply counting years of service or continuing education credits. Arbitrary measures like tenure or education credits may or may not have anything to do with being an insanely great teacher, but effectiveness in teaching children certainly does. Measuring academic results, especially for the hardest-to-teach students, is the only realistic way of fostering great teachers.

We should allow schools to hire qualified teachers from the broadest talent pool possible. Hiring great teachers has little to do with whether an applicant holds a teaching certificate. We should let school administrators avail themselves of other sources of teaching ability.

For example, only half of math and science teachers actually hold a college degree in math or science, yet state law bars a retired engineer with a Ph.D. from teaching algebra in a public high school (although such teachers are allowed in private schools). It makes no sense to force a retired mathematician to attend School of Education courses for 18 months just to get a teaching certificate, or to expect mid-career professionals to give up more than a year's salary to go back to school.

In addition to attracting top talent, constant and continual improvement should be a part of the teaching culture. In order for teachers to gain new skills, they need honest and constructive assessments of their work. As in other professional fields, frequent performance reviews should be the norm in teaching. Reviews should comprise both in-class observations as well as less frequent, but at least annual, formal performance reviews, especially in the early years of a teacher's career. These performance assessments should be the primary responsibility of the school principal.

Increasing the number of helping hands in the classroom can better leverage the teaching bandwidth that is already stretched thin. We should increase the number of adults in the classroom who can assist and complement the teacher. School leaders should be allowed to recruit interns, parents, volunteers, Teach for America, Teach Corps members and other creative sources of instructional talent to help students learn.

III

PLANK THREE:
THE FREEDOM TO CHOOSE

"The reason school choice succeeds is no mystery:
it gives power to the people who have the most at stake—parents."
JOHN O. NORQUIST, 37TH MAYOR OF MILWAUKEE

The following words describe the culture of the United States: freedom, diversity, democracy, free markets and equality before the law. Without these qualities, our country would lack the cultural environment that makes possible what we take for granted: a society that constantly strives for excellence and to provide opportunity for all.

The ability of citizens to choose what is best for their lives is central to the founding of our country and to the exercise of freedom. Our Constitution recognizes and protects our right to choose what we say, how we say it, where we meet, what we believe and the thousand other ways Americans express their freedom.

We choose our elected representatives in Congress. We even have the right to bear arms and choose not to quarter troops in our homes. The freedom to choose is also central to our free market economy, and to the principles of supply and demand. The benefits of competition apply to the non-profit sector as well. In the for-profit world, a key measure of success or failure is often how much profit was made that quarter. In the case of the public school system, where profit is not a motive, maximizing student learning should be used as the primary goal of people working in our schools.

As consumers, we can pick and choose based on any number of criteria that are important to us. We can choose based on price, style, availability, quality, quantity, responsiveness, customer service, brand name, location, or any other quality of value to us.

Yet when it comes to one of the most important decisions affecting the future of our children, their education, parental choice is often nonexistent in public schools. Parents are largely told where to send their child and what teacher the child will have. If a family lives in a neighborhood without a good public school the attitude of education officials is often…well, tough luck.

In contrast, no one would dream of accepting a system in which a government official assigned each citizen to use only the public gas station within two miles of his house, especially if the gas were underperforming and overpriced. And educating one's child is far more important than filling the gas tank.

We can barely imagine what life would be like in the United States if we applied the rigid lack of choice that exists in public education to other areas of life. When any company or government agency has a captive audience, the benefits of healthy market forces are lost. Without consumer choice, managers, whether public officials or company executives, have no incentive to innovate, improve quality, provide inspired leadership or create a culture of excellence.

If public school parents were allowed to choose where to send their children, and if principals were given control over school admissions, we would have the ingredients for bringing the benefits of free market competition to public education. Principals would be motivated to provide the very best education to children, so they could attract the best students.

Schools would likely begin to differentiate themselves in an effort to provide students with education options that do not exist today. Shaped by the "invisible hand" of market competition, this differentiation would take many forms. Some schools would focus on a science-based curriculum, others would focus on foreign language and international cultures.

Other schools might want to invest in advanced technology as a more predictable and reliable mode for teaching. Some schools would offer small class sizes or promote the benefits of study at a small school. Some schools might want to provide a gender-specific learning environment, creating unique learning environments for boys and girls.

Some schools might be project-based rather than using traditional course structures. Still others might want to be interdisciplinary in approach, offering classes that integrate the arts, philosophy, science and mathematics. Others might offer year-round courses. Some schools would adopt uniforms for students, while others might prefer to maintain an informal atmosphere in class. Ultimately, allowing choice among schools would provide parents with vast opportunities to provide for the education of their children based on factors that are important to them.

Parents must be *empowered* to send their children to the school of *their* choice. While I would like to believe that all parents would welcome the opportunity to seek out the schools that best align with their child's interests and learning style, not all parents will make informed choices. But the vast majority will. School administrators should avoid the mistake of a no-choice policy for everyone because a small minority will not take advantage of their best choices. If a small number of parents decide, for whatever reason, not to choose a school, their children are no worse off than they are now, since today most parents are not allowed to choose their child's school.

The obligations of parents

Freedom of choice in education should not be one-sided. While lawmakers should allow parents to have a choice among schools, school administrators should have some determination over which students to accept. Some schools might choose simply to take all children on a first-come, first-served basis. Other schools may be more selective. In either case, the admission criteria that school administrators could use would certainly be more varied than simply the home address of the student.

Other admissions criteria might include asking parents to sign a contract that lays out the school's expectations of involvement, including obligations like getting their children to school on time, insuring children start the day with a good breakfast, reading to their children in the evening, setting aside time for homework, insisting that extracurricular activities do not interfere with education fundamentals, helping with supplemental fundraising, volunteering at the school and ensuring their children respect the school's code of discipline.

For students who are not accepted at the school of their choice, public education officials would provide a safety net. The public system should provide sufficient capacity to ensure that every child gets into a school. This alternative could be managed through a lottery, in which the small number of kids who are not accepted at any of the schools to which they applied are given a place at an appropriate public school, perhaps the one closest to their homes. Alternatively, education officials may decide to create a number of regional "fall-back" schools that will guarantee admission to any child.

The freedoms associated with choice would lead to a profusion and richness of imaginative solutions that teachers, principals and school leaders could offer to best serve their respective communities' student populations.

IV

PLANK FOUR:
MORE TIME SPENT EDUCATING

"Make use of time, let not advantage slip."
WILLIAM SHAKESPEARE

There are many reasons why kids are not keeping pace as they progress through school. Those reasons include, but are in no way limited to, the student-to-teacher ratio, quality of instruction, quantity of instruction, pace of instruction, and duration of instruction.

Since current outcomes are falling far short of expectations, we should at least try to maximize the education returns of the human resources and the physical plant we are investing in, since these are somewhat fixed costs. Teachers are paid annually, yet they work far less than the 240 days of traditional salaried workers. Typically, public school teachers work about 180 days a year, minus employee discretionary days. What is magic about 180 days? Why not provide students with 240 instructional days, or some number in between?

In the past, when this country had an agriculturally-based economy, having as many able bodies available to tend to and harvest the crops dictated the school calendar. But children are no longer tied to the fields, and the 180-day school calendar is one of the restrictive outputs of the collective bargaining agreement.

If kids aren't learning given current instructional hours, then perhaps the number of hours they spend in the classroom each day should be lengthened. Another option would be to increase the number of classroom days in the school year. Children in Japan spend 35 percent more days in school than their American peers. Additionally, we should consider going to a year-round teaching calendar that evens out the current lumpiness of the teaching schedule. This raises the question, "Should teachers be paid more?" If student education outcomes improve dramatically, then yes, teachers should be paid more!

For those kids who are not performing to plan, common sense would say perhaps we should try all three options to increase in-class learning time: lengthen the school day, increase the number of school days, and go to a year-round teaching calendar. Kids who are performing to plan could participate in enrichment classes.

The efficacy of spending more time on task is well demonstrated. All else being equal, a child who spends ten hours learning multiplication tables will likely score higher than a child who spends one hour on the same task. A child who has practice sessions on the piano 240 days each year, will likely be more accomplished than a child who practices only 180 days each year. A child who practices a foreign language evenly through the year is likely to perform better than a child who studies a language for nine months and then takes the next three months off.

In addition to decreasing the inevitable backsliding that occurs when students take ten weeks off for summer vacation, there are other benefits to shifting to a year-round school calendar. Mini-break times throughout the year could be used for remedial work with children who are having difficulty with a particular subject. Teachers could use this time to work with Master Teachers to hone their skills, attend conferences, adjust lesson plans to meet the needs of their students, or enroll in university seminars that bring them up to date in their knowledge specialty.

In any case, lengthening the school day, increasing the number of teaching days in the school year, and/or adopting a year-round school calendar should be options available to school principals and their teaching teams, without first having to jump through complex bureaucratic hoops.

V

PLANK FIVE:
EARLY LEARNING RIGOR;
OPTIONAL HIGH SCHOOL

*"We know that what happens in the first five
years of a child's life has a huge amount of influence
on everything that happens afterwards."*
ED BALLS, BRITISH SECRETARY OF STATE,
DEPARTMENT OF CHILDREN, SCHOOLS AND FAMILIES

The importance of providing a safe, nurturing, healthy
environment for our very youngest children is well docu-
mented. Recent scientific studies show that ages birth to five
years are critical to the brain development of children. Brain
development in this age group is essential for kids to learn.
What we do (and equally important...don't do) will forever
shape their future and leave an imprint on all of society. We
know children learn more in their first five years than during
any other five year period in their lives.

Public schools offer kindergarten to all children, but attendance
is optional. An early warning signal of future educational
problems is the fact that only half of the children entering kindergarten are ready to learn. We should start even earlier than

kindergarten and offer programs and information to parents to ensure that all children are ready to be successful learners in kindergarten and beyond.

We must effect a systematic change in societal values and elevate the importance and commitment for parenting infants and toddlers. We must raise the bar and establish a new resolve in all parts of society to embrace the importance of an early learning environment that will optimize a child's ability to learn in kindergarten and instill skills that foster a lifetime of learning.

In addition to providing a strong foundation for learning, pre-school programs provide other societal benefits. Economist Robert Lynch in *Enriching Children, Enriching the Nation*, found that providing high-quality pre-school education produces large, measurable economic benefits for children and for society. The Lynch study estimates that the total annual budgetary, crime reduction and earnings benefits from a universal pre-school program in place nationwide would be $779 billion by 2050. For Washington state, the benefits are estimated to be $17.3 billion in 2050. This estimated annual benefit represents almost eight times the estimated yearly cost of the program.

Even if mandatory pre-school were implemented, we should also consider research focused on even earlier stages of development—zero to four years of age. Groundbreaking research by doctors Betty Hart and Todd Risley, *Meaningful Differences in the Everyday Experiences of Young American Children*, found that significant intellectual capacity is determined in the first 36 months of life. The authors report that a person's foundation for how they feel about themselves, self-esteem, is established in childhood and that lifelong intellectual curiosity is shaped in the earliest years. In fact, one of the most important findings of the Hart-Risley study puts conventional wisdom on its head.

Conventional wisdom might best be described as "success breeds success." Or, parents who are college graduates will have kids who will also graduate from college. Steven Levitt, in *Freakonomics*, states, "A child whose parents are highly educated typically does well in school; not much surprise there. A family with a lot of schooling tends to value schooling. Perhaps more important, parents with higher IQ's tend to get more education, and IQ is strongly hereditary." But, Dr. Clayton Christensen in his book, *Disrupting Class*, commented quite pointedly on the Hart-Risley study.

> "...the level of income, ethnicity, and level of parents' education had no explanatory power in determining the level of cognitive capacity that the children achieved. It is all explained by the amount of language dancing, or extra talk, over and above business talk, that the parents engage in. It accounted literally for all the variance in outcomes."

The amount of "language dancing" differences are profound. In the Hart-Risley study, "a child spoken to 50 times per hour will hear 700 utterances; a child spoken to 800 times per hour will hear more than 11,000 utterances."

If we extrapolate these differences over an entire year, the language exposure that a child receives can range from a low of 250,000 utterances to a high of four million utterances. According to the study, while the average four-year-old in a family receiving welfare has heard some 13 million spoken words, for example, a child from a working-class family has heard about 26 million, and a child from a professional family almost 45 million. "The amount of parenting per hour and the quality of the verbal content associated with that parenting, were strongly related to the subsequent IQ of the child." This is not an indictment of welfare families. It does, however, underscore that regardless of convenient class distinctions, if parents and caregivers would simply engage children in adult conversation with more frequency, children would be more intelligent than if not spoken to in this manner.

Opting out of High School

While I am a strong proponent for even earlier-than-kindergarten school programs and parental involvement, at the other end of the learning spectrum, I think we need to allow students (with their parents' approval) to opt out of a traditional high school education. Alternatives to formal high school include vocational training, trade or technical schools and occupational academies. We have to stop warehousing teenagers where the educational shelf life is quite limited, based on where we would like them to go (college), and get them into learning environments that are appropriate for their long-term goals. I believe many students will flourish if we engage them in classes they find meaningful, excite their interests and are relevant to their futures.

Why force a kid to endure a high school classroom environment when they have neither the desire nor the intention of going to college? That same student might be extremely excited to learn the skills required to be a journeyman welder or plumber, or a skilled carpenter. If a student is bored to tears learning Shakespeare, but comes alive in Auto Mechanics, how do we optimize the learning outcomes for that individual? We should place students in learning environments that are more closely aligned with their educational interests and career aspirations.

Each of these vocational tracks would still have to teach basic skills critical to the job. A carpenter or home builder would need to learn geometric concepts, like how to determine the slope of a line by measuring the pitch of a roof, or use algebraic formulae to determine how much plaster board to order to cover an irregularly shaped wall. A plumber would need to learn how the circumference of a pipe determines how much capacity that pipe can handle. Welders would need to know basic formulae for determining the area of a variety of geometric shapes as well as how to determine perimeter, volume and circumference.

These students would learn mathematics in a setting that is relevant to their trade. This kind of learning would no longer be an abstract exercise, but a relevant, practical one.

There are many examples of alternative tracks in high schools around the world. Germany has a multi-track secondary education system. University bound students are enrolled in *Gymnasiums*. Students with an aptitude and desire to learn a trade are enrolled in vocational schools called *Hauptschule*. England offers students a choice at age 14 of pursuing a course of study (A levels) that precedes entry to a university or an alternative path that leads to a technical school. Sweden's *Gymnasieskola* is bifurcated into studies for higher ed or vocational education. Japan has an extremely competitive university track for high school students or the option of pursuing technical or vocational training through *Senmon Gakkou*. In New Zealand, students can opt out of a high school college track for entry into a vocational institute.

With education, we are dealing with the most precious output of all...the ability of our children to live productive lives and contribute to society in a positive way. We must apply more discipline and rigor in making the tough resource allocation decisions in the earliest years so that children have a chance to excel in the field of their choice in later years. While the U.S. public school system is currently focused on getting kids graduated from high school and into college, we should take more care to understand what high school aged kids really want and provide alternative tracks that are more attuned to their aspirations.

VI

PLANK SIX:
MUSTER AN ARMY
OF VOLUNTEERS

*"A lot of people have gone further than they thought
they could because someone else thought they could."*
UNKNOWN

We should supplement the one-to-many, in-class teaching paradigm with a one-to-one educational approach which involves parents. Parents are a child's first caregivers, and they should not abdicate their primary responsibility (a big part of which is education) to the "system." Parents should be encouraged to become more involved in education to ensure the proper learning outcomes for their children. Parents are much more than providers of food, shelter, and safety. Parents are teachers of their children, and can meaningfully contribute to learning by checking homework, reading to young children, asking questions, engaging kids in conversation, and the thousand other ways parents create a stimulating learning environment at home.

Mentors can also play a critical role as part-time, substitute parents. This is clearly reinforced by the impact they can have on kids in a one-to-one relationship (Big Brothers and Big Sisters, Friends of Children, Rainier Scholars); a one-to-a-few relationship (Summer Search, Seattle Scores); or a one-to-many environment (Boy Scouts, Girl Scouts, "Y" Guides). Children could gain access to learning mentors through a social networking software application. This could be a highly leveraged use of technology.

Tutors can focus attention on specific subject matter difficulties. The use of peer tutors—students helping students—should be employed in a much broader way. Students who excel in a particular subject matter offer an excellent educational resource available to work one-on-one with a peer who is having difficulty. Team READ, a non-profit group that provides student tutors for children who are not reading at grade level, is a great example of this approach. Team READ produces stellar results by using high school students who are paid to teach second and third graders. A reduced cost model is currently being tested to see if the use of unpaid fifth and sixth grade students or middle school peer tutors works as well. Another alternative would be to "pay" these middle school tutors by letting them earn money that is put into a college savings account.

In 1961, President Kennedy created the Peace Corps. Why couldn't President Obama create a Teach Corps? The purpose of Teach Corps would be to create an army of volunteers who would work in classrooms around the country to assist teachers in any number of ways. "Army" is a good descriptive word in this case. To put this in perspective, the combined strength of the U.S. Regular Army, the U.S. Army National Guard, and the U.S. Army Reserve numbers just over one million personnel. The number of members in the American Association of Retired Persons is over 35 million! AARP's Washington State Chapter alone has almost one million members. If only a fraction of AARP members expressed interest in helping students, the amount of knowledge and learning available for classroom instruction would increase tremendously.

These volunteers could potentially be recruited from the large number of baby boomer retirees, from the ranks of corporate America, where companies could "loan" employees for one or two years. High school students spending a gap year before going to college could help in K-12 classrooms, as could college graduates wanting to help fix the public schools before committing themselves to their lifelong careers.

Another source of teaching talent is corporate alumni organizations, many of which have tens of thousands of members who are retired and still actively engaged in many other affinity groups. Most of these Teach Corps volunteers could focus initially on assisting teachers in the earliest grades and in schools that are not performing well. If there is additional volunteer capacity, it can be deployed in accordance with the priorities of the school district.

VII

PLANK SEVEN: STANDARDIZED CURRICULUM... NOT

"Instead of a national curriculum for education,
what is really needed is an individual curriculum for every child."
CHARLES HANDY, IRISH AUTHOR AND PHILOSOPHER

W hen it comes to education, one size does not fit all. Despite our highly-industrialized modern society, there is no way to automate learning. Even today, every child's education should be hand-crafted, with knowledge patiently passed from the teacher to the mind of the student.

We should not forget that the student is the customer. This will likely require a significant on-going investment to revise existing curricula and to create a wide variety of the absolutely best teaching methods for each subject that can serve as the antidote to any symptoms of torpor in the classroom. We should allow principals and teachers to select the curriculum that best fits the needs of their particular students. We should spend the necessary funds to produce the best algebra course or the best western history course, as needed. These curricula should be both academically rigorous and high on the fun quotient. Most importantly, different curriculum approaches need to recognize that students learn differently; that pace of learning varies from child to child, and; that there is likely not just one way that will work for everyone.

Policymakers should take extreme care when considering whether the use of technology is appropriate for advancing a school's education mission. Today's technology is expensive to acquire, expensive to maintain and expensive to replace because of its rapid obsolescence. However, if a principal and his team decide that the investment in technology is justified, there are some exciting developments to consider.

An appropriate use of technology would be on-line instruction that uses an adaptive curriculum. A big advantage to using technology in this way is teaching can be customized to the learning needs of each child. The pace of learning can be varied. Teachers can individually tailor the way that learning occurs. Perhaps the biggest reason to use adaptive instruction is to adjust learning modalities and exercises when the learning software shows the student is having difficulty with the material.

Computers with adaptive curriculum software that are deployed in the very earliest grades are probably more useful than computers used in the higher grades if only because critical thinking is so much more advanced, nuanced, creative and unpredictable in the later years.

Trends in technology offer glimpses of a bright future with a cornucopia of potential applications that can affect learning, both within and outside of a classroom setting, as well as administrative applications that can help with data acquisition and analysis. Computer technology will be more powerful and less expensive going forward. Place-bound technology (desktop computers) will be supplanted by mobile technology (cell phones, small appliances). Technology focused on individual learning will be complemented with technology focused on community learning. These social networks will be beneficial to students interacting with other students, students interacting with teachers, and teachers interacting with other teachers. Gaming algorithms will help make learning fun.

While managed instruction strategies are ideal for the earliest grades, more freedom and flexibility in pedagogical approaches is necessary for the higher grades. This will be required if only because of the increasing complexity of critical thinking skills as children mature, and because programs will have to be adapted to the particular focus of the school. These student-centered schools will have to design academic programs to match student interests.

Focus on curriculum content

What exactly should be taught in our public schools? Should
the focus be on breadth of knowledge or on depth of learning? Should we have an infinite variety of subjects, or should
we focus in-depth on a handful of targeted areas? In some
instances, limited school budgets and the No Child Left Behind
Act have helped decide in the favor of knowledge depth, with
fewer subjects being taught.

In many schools music and art classes have been largely eliminated. Given this narrowing approach, what subject is next on
the chopping block? Foreign language? Physical education?
Sports programs? Sex education? While you and I may believe
all of these subjects are important, they may not be essential. In
our desire to provide a well-rounded, comprehensive education,
we have so much variety in subject matter that the overarching
goal of the curriculum—to produce well-educated students—
has become ineffectual. We should return to a more focused
approach, with more class time devoted to a smaller number of
essential subjects. Even though the breadth of subjects would
be more limited, we should embrace many different ways to
teach the same material.

A good example of this is a program called First Move, created
by the non-profit organization, America's Foundation for
Chess (AF4C). First Move uses chess as a vehicle to impact

higher-level analytical thinking skills and to improve the learning outcomes in the areas of math and reading for second and third grade students. An unanticipated outcome was the behavioral changes in the students that were noticed by the teachers. Students became more courteous, with less acting-up in and out of the classroom. Here are a few results of a survey of First Move teachers conducted at the end of the 2007 school year:

- 100 percent of teachers believe their students find First Move engaging;
- 94 percent of teachers believe First Move is a valuable use of classroom time;
- 90 percent of teachers would highly recommend First Move to other schools and teachers;
- 88 percent of teachers believe their students' higher-level thinking skills increased due to First Move.

I believe a more focused curriculum is critical for students on the trailing edge of the performance gap. There can certainly be more variety, intensity and flexibility in the curriculum for high-performing students. But let us not forget that the ultimate decision to have a focused (depth) or a highly varied (breadth) curriculum should be the decision of each school's principal and its Board of Directors.

What should be the role and focus for our public school system in educating our youth? Fundamentally, what does it mean to be an educated person? I'll leave the complete answers to the experts. There probably are no final answers. As a practical minimum, upon leaving school our children need to be literate, with strong working knowledge of spoken and written English, to have mastery of mathematics (including geometry and algebra, though trigonometry and calculus are probably overkill), to understand the natural world, to grasp the core concepts of science, to understand how democracy works, and to know the history of their country, region and state. Most importantly, at the end of their K-12 school journey, all students should be able to do one thing: think critically. Many of the very best critical thinkers will go on to be further challenged and have their thinking refined in our institutions of higher learning.

VIII
PLANK EIGHT:
EARLY INTERVENTION AND
SPECIALIZED INSTRUCTION

"An ounce of prevention is worth a pound of cure."
BENJAMIN FRANKLIN, *POOR RICHARD'S ALMANAC*

We should work early with kids who show the first sign of learning difficulties in school. Education leaders should focus on immediate, micro-remedial action to help these children, by putting in place tutoring and mentoring services for kids who fall behind. Summer and vacation times should be used, as needed, to provide catch-up classes for lagging students.

Most urgently, school administrators should stop the insanity of social promotion—advancing students to the next grade when they are academically unprepared—all in the name of preserving their self-esteem, or perhaps simply because it happens to be easier than addressing the child's real learning needs.

Never let a defect pass on to the next station. Many of the world's best manufacturing companies practice this basic tenet of quality control. Industry leaders know from hard experience that if defects are not identified and solved, the long-term costs to repair, maintain and re-design a product become exorbitant. In the case of education, social promotion from one grade to the next only results in harming the student, who then suffers from a continuous lack of competency in tackling ever-increasing complex subject matter. Worse, social promotion only dilutes a classroom filled with kids ready and anxious to learn with unprepared, unmotivated students placed there by administrators who know these students lack the requisite skills.

The result is "least common denominator" learning, in which the teacher is forced to lower the rigor of the day's lesson to the level of the least prepared student, or else condemn that student to falling even further behind his peers. This approach to learning makes little sense. Nor does diverting precious teacher time and resources from kids who are fully capable of learning and allocating them to what often amounts to in-class babysitting and disciplinary chores.

In the early preK-4 grades, public schools should focus on getting kids reading at grade level. Reading is the gateway to learning, and the inability to read creates a cascade effect across the curriculum. If a child cannot read at grade level, he will have difficulty with every other subject that involves reading. Even in math, story problems and exam instructions require students to have a clear understanding of how written words convey meaning.

As mentioned previously, programs like Team READ use paid high school student tutors, as well as unpaid peer tutors, after school to help struggling students improve their reading skills, so they are better prepared for the next day's classes. The results are dramatic.

Maureen Massey, Executive Director for Team READ, reports the following program results for 430 second and third graders for the 2006-2007 school year: 90 percent were students of color; 85 percent were eligible for free or reduced lunch; 45 percent of student readers were English Language Learners. All student cohorts showed marked improvement from working with Team READ tutors.

For second grade students, 68 percent of students were reading significantly below grade level before Team READ interventional tutoring. "Significant" is defined as reading one to 1.5 grade levels below second grade level. After one year of tutoring, the trend was reversed, and 63 percent of second graders were reading at or above grade level.

For third grade students, 32 percent were reading significantly below grade level at the start of the year. This third grade group also experienced significant gains. After one year of Team READ tutoring, 55 percent of third graders who started the year reading below grade level were reading at or above grade level.

This certainly represents a lot of work by the second and third grade students to conquer the mechanics of reading. One can only hope that they will fall in love with reading. They are off to a good start...80 percent of second and third graders said that reading was more fun since joining Team READ. The results were noticed by parents and teachers as well. Ninety-four percent of the parents of the second and third graders and 95 percent of their teachers reported increased reading skills as a result of participation in Team READ. Programs like this can have a positive influence on the common learning challenges that many students face.

Education leaders should devote particular attention to special needs kids, if only because the numbers continue to grow each year. Consider these data points:

• Nationally, the National Center for Education Statistics reports that the percentage of kids served under the Individuals with Disabilities Education Act was 8.6 percent in 2006. This represents almost 6.7 million children with learning disabilities. [http://nces.ed.gov/pubs2008/nativetrends/tables/table_2_3a.asp]

• Statewide, the Office of the Superintendent of Public Instruction (OSPI) reports that the percentage of kids in special education in May 2008 was 12.6 percent or 130,000 children. [http://reportcard.ospi.k12.wa.us/summary.aspx?year=2007-08]

•Seattle Public Schools have 13.9 percent of kids in special education. The Bellevue School District is at 10.7 percent. Tacoma School District is at 13.3 percent. Federal Way is 13.0 percent.

The term "special needs" covers a wide range of conditions: specific learning disabilities like ADHD, speech or language impairment, emotional disturbance, mental retardation, autism, orthopedic impairment, hearing impairment or deafness, visual impairment or blindness, or traumatic brain injury. Addressing special needs kids is fast becoming an enormous challenge because of the growing number of children afflicted with these conditions, and because the federal government does not fully fund the cost of a "free appropriate" education. In many cases this cost is two, three and even ten times more expensive than the cost to educate a non-special needs child.

Should special needs children be addressed in a segregated manner that is targeted to their particular needs, or should they be mainstreamed in larger classrooms where teachers are ill-equipped to address these students' special requirements? Take the case of autism:

> "Experts disagree on the most effective approach to teaching children with autism, and many school districts cobble together a mishmash of methods that changes with each new fad, source of funding, special education director, or classroom teacher. Too often, good intentions collide with limited resources, and overloaded bureaucracies clash with parents driven by hope and anguish. The result is often a mess." [Fran Smith, Edutopia, Overcoming Autism: Public Schools Deal with a Growing Problem, 2008.]

Children who are mentally disabled should be taught by specialists who are trained to deal with their learning challenges. Children who are deaf or blind should be placed in centers where experts can address their unique needs. Placing them in mainstream schools is a disservice to them because the teachers are not prepared for them and it is unfair to the other students.

Children of immigrant families that enter public schools and are unable to read or speak English should be immersed for a year in schools that focus solely on teaching the English language. The sooner these children have a command of English, the sooner they can enter and excel in the mainstream public school system. Failing to teach them English quickly condemns children of immigrants to falling further and further behind in school, and risks isolating them from participating fully in the social and economic life of their adopted country.

We can all agree that every child should have access to a public education. This societal goal is reflected in the law. Whether the more effective means to accomplish this is by segregation or by integration is much debated. I believe the answer is: It depends on each individual case. If a child, whether handicapped or not, is a distraction to the rest of the classroom, that child should be removed from the classroom and placed in a separate environment. The school can then provide that student with more focused and effective attention and specialized resources.

IX

PLANK NINE:
SPEND MONEY AS THOUGH
IT WERE YOUR OWN

*"The worst, the hardest, the most disagreeable thing that you may
have to do may be the only thing that counts most, because it is the hard
discipline, and it alone, that makes possible the highest efficiency."*
ELIHU ROOT, AMERICAN LAWYER AND STATESMAN,
NOBEL PRIZE FOR PEACE IN 1912

In more than a few ways, this is where the rubber meets the
road. Before we invest a few billion dollars more each year to
try to improve our public schools, I believe we first need to start
by assiduously looking at every dollar we currently spend and
decide if it is absolutely necessary. Then, for those line items
that we feel cannot be cut or eliminated, we need to determine
if there is a more effective and/or efficient way to achieve those
respective goals and objectives.

We must disentangle existing public education funding so more
resources go to carrying out each school's core mission: educating children. Directing more of the public education budget to
the core mission means that class sizes can be decreased, teaching and counseling resources can be devoted to students, and

more administrative flexibility can improve learning outcomes. Freeing up existing education funding means taking a cold, hard look at each line item in the education budget. How careful are school administrators when spending existing taxpayer dollars? Have they eliminated activities that do not advance their core mission? Have they taken advantage of contracting out to secure for schools the best products and services at the best price? Contracting out non-essential services allows schools to get the best from firms whose very existence requires they be the most efficient providers of their respective product or service.

Of the $9 billion spent on K-12 education in Washington state, only a small fraction finds its way to the classroom. Along the way from the state capitol in Olympia to the schoolhouse door, there are too many Big Bad Wolves taking bites from the funding pie. The largest bites are taken by central school district administrative overhead, transportation and food service. These three areas account for $1.73 billion. The Office of Superintendent of Public Instruction takes another $77 million bite.

We must figure out how to manage the business of public education without the costly administrative burden that is currently in place. We are the only country in the world where non-teaching administrative positions exceeds the number of teaching positions. Countries such as Japan, France, Belgium and Australia employ four teachers for every non-teaching employee. It seems only school systems in the United States employ more non-teachers than teachers! Why does the state of Washington have 295 school districts? In the for-profit world, such a huge number of administrative divisions would offer a great opportunity to save money through roll-up and consolidation.

It is interesting to note the sheer number of non-teaching jobs in the Seattle Public School system. Here are a few:

SUPERINTENDENT, CHIEF ACADEMIC OFFICER, CHIEF FINANCIAL OFFICER, DIRECTOR OF EQUITY, RACE & LEARNING SUPPORT, EQUITY AND RACE RELATIONS SPECIALIST, DISTRICT MANAGER OF VISUAL AND PERFORMING ARTS, EXECUTIVE DIRECTOR OF CURRICULUM & INSTRUCTION, LEAD DIRECTOR OF INSTRUCTION, DIRECTOR OF SPECIAL EDUCATION, DIRECTOR OF SCHOOL IMPROVEMENT, DIRECTOR OF SUPPORT, PREVENTION AND INTERVENTION, GENERAL COUNSEL , EXECUTIVE DIRECTOR OF HUMAN RESOURCES, DIRECTOR OF INSTRUCTIONAL SERVICES, PROGRAM MANAGER FOR LITERACY, PROGRAM MANAGER FOR VISUAL & PERFORMING ARTS, PROGRAM MANAGER FOR MATHEMATICS, PROGRAM MANAGER FOR PHYSICAL EDUCATION, PROGRAM MANAGER FOR BILINGUAL SERVICES, SUPERVISOR OF HEALTH EDUCATION, INTERNATIONAL EDUCATION ADMINISTRATOR, PROFESSIONAL DEVELOPMENT PROGRAM MANAGER, OFFICE MANAGER, SENIOR ADMINISTRATIVE ASSISTANT, PLC PROGRAM SPECIALIST, PROGRAM MANAGER FOR SCIENCE, COORDINATOR OF SMALL LEARNING COMMUNITIES, PROFESSIONAL GROWTH & EVALUATION PROJECT COORDINATOR, COORDINATOR OF PARAEDUCATORS, SAEOP, AND SUBSTITUTE EDUCATORS, MIGRANT ED/COMMUNITY LIAISON, ELEMENTARY HEALTH & PreK-12 SPECIAL EDUCATION, HS HEALTH & PreK-12 DIVERSITY, ESL HEALTH

ED SPECIALIST, INSTRUCTIONAL MATERIALS SPECIALIST, SCIENCE
MATERIALS CENTER – MANAGER, SCIENCE MATERIALS CENTER–
ASSISTANT, DIRECTOR OF COMMUNICATIONS AND PUBLIC AFFAIRS,
DIRECTOR OF STRATEGIC PLANNING AND ALLIANCES, DIRECTOR OF
RESEARCH, EVALUATION & ASSESSMENT, DIRECTOR OF TECHNOLOGY
SERVICES, DIRECTOR OF SCHOOL SUPPORT SERVICES, DIRECTOR
OF WAREHOUSE, MAIL, PURCHASING AND CONTRACTS, DIRECTOR
OF POLICY AND GOVERNMENT RELATIONS, DIRECTOR OF BUDGET,
DIRECTOR OF ACCOUNTING, DIRECTOR OF INTERNAL AUDITING,
DIRECTOR OF FISCAL COMPLIANCE AND GRANTS, DIRECTOR OF
SUPPORT, PREVENTION AND INTERVENTION, DIRECTOR OF ENROLLMENT
AND PLANNING, DIRECTOR OF SCHOOL IMPROVEMENT, MANAGER &
EEOC OFFICER, MANAGER EMPLOYEE AND LABOR RELATIONS TEAM
1, MANAGER EMPLOYEE AND LABOR RELATIONS TEAM 2, MANAGER
EMPLOYEE AND LABOR RELATIONS TEAM 3, MANAGER EMPLOYMENT
TEAM 4, RECRUITER, MANAGER PAYROLL TEAM 5, RETIREMENT
SPECIALIST, MANAGER CLASS/COMP, BENEFITS, LEAVE, HRIS & SUB
OFFICE TEAM 6, HRIS SPECIALIST, HRIS LEAVE SPECIALIST, LEAVE
ADMINISTRATOR, SUPERVISOR EMPLOYEE ASSISTANCE PROGRAM,
COUNSELOR, OCCUPATIONAL THERAPIST, SCHOOL PSYCHOLOGIST,
OCCUPATIONAL PHYSICAL THERAPIST, DIRECTOR OF LABOR RELATIONS,
LEAD HR DATA ANALYST, INFO SERVICES PROJECT MANAGER III (I
ASSUME THERE IS ALSO A I AND II, MAYBE A IV AND V?), PROGRAM
EVALUATOR, DRUG/ALCOHOL INTERVENTION SPECIALIST, BILINGUAL
INST. ASST. – TAGALOG, BILINGUAL INST. ASST. – SOMALI, BILINGUAL
INST. ASST. – CHINESE, BILINGUAL INST. ASST. – KOREAN, BILINGUAL
INST. ASST. – VIETNAMESE, BILINGUAL INST. ASST. – SPANISH, DATA
REGISTRATION ASSISTANT, HIGH SCHOOL FISCAL SPECIALIST, ON-CALL
CUSTODIAN, GARDENER, BUDGET ANALYST I, BUDGET ANALYST II,
HEADSTART AREA SUPERVISOR, SPEECH AND LANGUAGE PATHOLOGIST,
SCHOOL TO WORK SPECIALIST, TYPE II DL COORDINATOR,
INSTRUCTIONAL SERVICE MUSIC COACH, INSTRUCTIONAL SERVICE
SCHOOL COACH, INSTRUCTIONAL SERVICE BILINGUAL SCHOOL COACH,
CHILDREN SERVICES COORDINATOR, FAMILY SERVICE COORDINATOR.
Okay, enough already.

Do we really need all of these non-teaching positions? I am not trying to pick on Seattle, but since it is the largest and most diverse school district in our state, it naturally attracts attention. The total number of staff on the Seattle Public Schools (SPS) payroll is 5,028. Over 10 percent of SPS' annual budget is contracted out, which represents about 500 full-time-equivalent employees. The total number of teachers on the payroll is about 2,548. This means we have more non-teachers than teachers supporting the education of our children! If you believe, as I do, that learning occurs in the classroom with an insanely great teacher at the helm, then surely we need some serious re-thinking on labor apportionment.

Totally eliminating or contracting out non-essential services would free up significant capital. Why are public schools in the transportation business? It seems to me that it is the responsibility of parents to get their children to school and get them back home at the end of the school day. Parents can walk their children to school, drive them to school, use public transportation, or arrange for a car pool with other parents. Taking responsibility to get their children to class each day is common among private, parochial school parents, many of whom are low and middle-income working people, just like public school parents. High schools could insist, for example, that if a student wants a parking pass, he must agree to offer a ride each day to other students. For each full-time position that can be eliminated in providing transportation, another teacher can be hired for the classroom.

Why are public schools in the food service business? Well, we know the answer to this. One cannot deny the fact that if a child is hungry, he is less able to concentrate in the classroom. But shouldn't parents have the responsibility to feed their child each morning before they go to school, to make a brown bag lunch, and to feed them a healthy meal for dinner? Private, parochial school parents do this every day. Schools could provide easy-to-service items such as juice and milk, fresh fruit and healthy snack bars; but, being in the full-service food business is not part of a school's mission when educating our children. Making sure kids are fed fits more appropriately with the mission and responsibility of the welfare system. Let the welfare system focus on the social safety net. Let the education system focus on education.

The annual costs of transportation and food service in Washington state's public schools exceeds $600 million each year! This amount of money would go a long way toward reducing the shortage of qualified teachers, especially in math and science, would decrease class sizes, would allow higher salaries for new teachers (thereby attracting better candidates to the teaching profession), and would make funds available to principals for the professional development of their teaching staff. This would allow principals to pursue continuous improvement by investing in human capital.

While transportation and food service costs represent a significant piece of the expense pie, there are many more categories that should be looked at. Nurses, therapists, security, janitorial, clerical and administrative positions should all be evaluated by each school principal. They are the ones in a position to best apply the necessary rigor when evaluating all aspects of school spending. These principals can make the hard trade-offs between more security or lower student-to-teacher ratios. They can decide between more clerical and administrative costs or more funding for the professional development of the teaching team.

Eliminate the costs that are associated with the Washington Assessment of Student Learning (WASL) and other testing to see whether our children can actually read, write and do arithmetic. If we let capitalism work, it would soon be clear which schools are producing students who have the learning outcomes that middle schools, high schools and colleges demand. Each school could devise its own admissions criteria and tests. Each school could also go through a rigorous, periodic accreditation process conducted by a team of experts and peer principals. Another alternative to the WASL would be a system of yearly matriculation. Students would have to pass subject tests before being allowed to proceed to the next grade level.

X

PLANK TEN:
PLANT THE SEEDS OF
SUCCESS IN LIFE: VALUES,
CHARACTER, LEADERSHIP

"Sow an act...reap a habit;
Sow a habit...reap a character;
Sow a character...reap a destiny."
GEORGE DANA BOARDMAN

One of the most troubling aspects of society today is the seeming disintegration of our moral backbone. Without a concerted effort to establish values, mold character, and develop leadership skills at the earliest ages, we will continue to be plagued by all manner of societal problems. Schools should nurture strength of character starting in pre-school, and continue to develop it in students through high school. In public school, learning life skills should be just as important as learning the three R's. It should be an integral part of each child's learning experience.

Some of the most effective programs that help develop strength of character already exist. We simply need to have all children participating in these programs, either as part of the curriculum, or as a required after school activity, or both. Girl Scouts and Boy Scouts are examples of youth programs that offer permanent and enduring life lessons.

Imagine for a moment every girl graduating from middle school having earned the highest distinction the Girl Scouts of America gives to qualified girls, the Gold Award. Imagine for a moment every boy graduating from middle school having earned the highest distinction the Boy Scouts of America gives to qualified boys, the Eagle Award.

I am particularly fond of Boy Scouts. I am an Eagle Scout. My two sons are Eagle Scouts. I am working to convince the National Boy Scouts of America to allow girls to earn this distinction. Growing up as an inner city kid in Seattle, scouting was one of those activities that, in hindsight, had a profound effect on my life.

We had buckets full of challenges and adventure. We learned how to take care of ourselves. We learned about the importance of taking care of others, especially those less fortunate. We rejoiced in the camaraderie of our patrol members and the importance of inclusion. We interacted with adult mentors (Scoutmasters, merit badge counselors, camp rangers) on a regular basis. We learned first-hand the wonders of nature and our responsibility to preserve those wonders for future generations. We learned to explore and to be creative problem solvers. We learned to follow and we learned to lead. I know this process of self-discovery, though it is not the exclusive domain of Scouting, made me a more conscientious student in the classroom.

The bedrock of the Boy Scout program has not changed in over 100 years. Its focus on values, character and leadership, and the equally important goal of establishing a pattern of accomplishment for kids, remain key elements of the scouting program.

That pattern starts with baby steps as a Tenderfoot Scout and proceeds up ever more challenging terrain all the way to the summit of Eagle Scout. If we could get every kid to accomplish this, we just might eliminate many of society's ailments. We would see juvenile crime rates plummet. We would see high school graduation rates soar. We would see and benefit from the heightened self-esteem, self-confidence, and leadership qualities these kids would possess.

I have arrived at the conclusion that the $120 per year per kid spent in Scouting to build character, establish a value system, and develop leadership skills is a far better investment than the $40,000 it costs taxpayers to keep one inmate in prison for a year. Even more sobering is the fact that if you count the people on probation and parole, there are more people in the penal system than there are pursuing baccalaureate degrees in our nation's public universities! It makes me wonder which would we rather have shaping our future.

XI

PLANK ELEVEN: ESTABLISH A CULTURE OF EXCELLENCE

"We are what we repeatedly do.
Excellence, then, is not an act, but a habit."
ARISTOTLE

An organization's culture is the critical element in the successful execution of strategy. It is the binding agent that makes everything hold together. Becoming the best at something at a point in time requires a lot of blood, sweat and tears. Staying the best over a long period of time requires a culture that is imbedded with enormous amounts of "excellence DNA."

This "excellence DNA" takes many forms: open and honest communication; teamwork; the elimination of bureaucracy; a shared vision and passion for the work to be done; a unified view of wanting to be the best; a commitment to constant improvement; the elimination of the attitude, "That's not my job."

Applied to the world of education, "excellence DNA" might reveal itself in the following ways: a focus on delivering the best education product to the customer; individuals who are empowered and take ownership for their respective roles, and "Level 5 leaders" at the key posts of Superintendent of Public Instruction, superintendent of schools for each school district, and principal for each school.

In his book, *Good to Great*, Jim Collins defines a Level 5 leader, and what differentiates an individual at the highest level of the executive hierarchy from a Level 1 leader at the bottom:

> "A Level 1 leader (Highly Capable Individuals) makes productive contributions through talent, knowledge, skills, and good work habits. A Level 5 executive builds enduring greatness through a paradoxical blend of personal humility and professional will." [Jim Collins, *Good to Great*, New York: HarpersCollins Publishers Inc., 2001, pg. 20.]

Collins suggests that a firm cannot be great without Level 5 leaders. If you have them, keep them. If you don't have them, find them (they are often already within your own company or system).

A culture of excellence won't happen overnight. Toyota Motor Company is world renown for The Toyota Way, a culture based on continuous improvement and respect for people. Their system is rooted in the very basic approach of challenging everything, all the time. The Toyota Way is being emulated by large and small companies, manufacturers and service businesses, in diverse industries, at home and abroad. Gary Convis, President of Toyota Motor Manufacturing in Kentucky, describes it this way:

> "More important than the actual improvements that individuals contribute, the true value of continuous improvement is in creating an atmosphere of continuous learning and an environment that not only accepts but actually embraces change. Such an environment can only be created where there is respect for people."

Is there a home for this culture in our public school education system? If so, a culture of excellence in public education will not happen overnight. It will be a journey that will require everyone to embrace change and relentlessly pursue innovation and the constant refinement of ideas. It will require a mindset of being problem solvers rather than problem creators. It will mean being focused on doing the right things and being religious about not doing the wrong things.

A culture of excellence in public education would make demands on many constituents. Students would be expected to do their homework and come to class prepared to learn. School faculty must be passionate about teaching every minute of every day. Principals must lead by example. They must inspire everyone involved in the education of the children in their care.

Parents must be willing and active participants in the education of their children. Politicians must prioritize education ahead of many other pressing needs. The community needs to embrace the costs (taxes) associated with delivering excellence in education. Administrators must be maniacal about weeding out all unnecessary spending.

If we work independently, no matter how diligently, it will only lead to the continuing decay of our public school system. If we all work together toward a common goal and with a unified plan, we can start on the long, arduous path to greatness and an education system that will build a brighter future for everyone.

FIXING THE PUBLIC SCHOOL
EDUCATION SYSTEM

"There are risks and costs to a program of action. But they are far less than the long-range risks and costs of comfortable inaction."
JOHN F. KENNEDY

How can we come to an agreement of what is the unified view of the problem? How do we marshal our resources in a manner that leads to systemic improvement in our public school education system?

The task of working with the various stakeholders to agree on the problem definition is best handled in an informal way. A special czar or czarina could be appointed by the governor to provide the critical leadership needed to bring common sense to the table. Trust will be a mandatory ingredient. Give-and-take discussions will have to be held in strict confidence. As soon as this process becomes public, open and honest communications will abate since political agendas will influence the dialogue.

Assuming we can get everyone involved in education to agree on the problem as outlined above (with anticipated modifications), coalitions can be formed to attack portions of the problem in a coordinated fashion. Those with an interest in public education are significant and numerous, each with their own agenda. However, we must all put aside narrow self-interest for the benefit of the common good. Politicians, school boards, school administrative staffs, principals and their unions/associations, teachers and their unions, corporations, parents, volunteers, students, schools of higher education, private and public foundations, education-focused non-profit entities, and other youth-serving agencies all have to come together to embrace the enormity of the task at hand.

More than a few people have commented that there are too many planks in this manifesto (even God only issued ten commandments). Though they agree with the contents, these pundits warn that many readers might have difficulty comprehending so many elements to education reform. In the world of business, I have always had a penchant for the benefits of focus, focus, focus. In an effort to capture all the rays of light, then concentrate and amplify those rays into a laser beam, I offer the following prescription to achieve the focus needed to improve our education system.

Freedom of choice should be the rallying cry for everyone involved in education. If we focus on the power of choice, we can open the floodgates of innovation and change in virtually all areas. Parents should have the freedom to send their children to a school that, in their opinion, best fits the needs of their child and family. Teachers should have the freedom to choose how to teach. Principals should have the freedom to choose who is on their team, how to allocate their school budgets and how to create the best learning environment for their students.

Corporate leaders can choose to focus their community citizenship by providing "loaned executives" or urging their employees and alumni to assist in the classroom. Politicians can choose to allow innovation by changing the education budget formula to one where funding follows the child. Teachers' unions can choose to replace the rigid "time and credits" salary formula with an alternative that rewards teachers based on merit and performance. School superintendents can choose to allow their principals the freedom to make decisions that fit their schools, rather than imposing top-down, one-size-fits-all regulations.

Four areas of choice

Choice can be applied at four basic levels: to students, to the classroom, to the school, and to the school community. Think of these four elements radiating outward in concentric circles, with the student in the center.

I believe that if we concentrate our efforts first on the student (after all, they are the customers) and then work our way outward, we will see tangible results in improving academic outcomes in public schools. At the same time, we must resist the temptation to think that if we focus only on one area we can fix public education. The problem is much bigger than that, and we will be sorely disappointed if we do not address what happens in all four areas.

The student. Although it is easy to think of students as a homogeneous group, we should actually think of students in the singular and individual sense. Each and every student has a unique personality, unique strengths and weaknesses, unique learning styles and unique interests. While it would be far too expensive to address these unique elements in a one-to-one student-to-teacher ratio, we must also resist the tendency to teach to the lowest common denominator.

It is interesting that the Individuals with Disabilities Education Act mandates that special needs students have an Individual Education Plan, an IEP. We should take heed and apply similar specificity to the education for all students and not just to special needs students.

As a tiny portion of the Act states:

> "The term `individualized education program' or `IEP' means a written statement for each child with a disability that is developed, reviewed, and revised in accordance with this section and that includes—(I) a statement of the child's present levels of academic achievement and functional performance, includ-

ing—(aa) how the child's disability affects the child's involvement and progress in the general education curriculum;(bb) for preschool children, as appropriate, how the disability affects the child's participation in appropriate activities; and,(cc) for children with disabilities who take alternate assessments aligned to alternate achievement standards, a description of benchmarks or short-term objectives;(II) a statement of measurable annual goals, including academic and functional goals, designed to—(aa) meet the child's needs that result from the child's disability to enable the child to be involved in and make progress in the general education curriculum; and (bb) meet each of the child's other educational needs that result from the child's disability; (III) a description of how the child's progress toward meeting the annual goals described in subclause (II) will be measured and when periodic reports on the progress the child is making toward meeting the annual goals(such as through the use of quarterly or other periodic reports, concurrent with the issuance of report cards) will be provided;(IV) a statement of the special education and related services and supplementary aids and services, based on peer-reviewed research to the extent practicable, to be provided to the child, or on behalf of the child, and a statement of the program modifications or supports for school personnel that will be provided for the child—(aa) to advance appropriately toward attaining the annual goals;(bb) to be involved in and make progress in the general education curriculum in accordance with subclause (I) and to participate in extracurricular and other nonacademic activities; and (cc) to be educated and participate with other children with disabilities and nondis abled children in the activities described in this subparagraph; (V) an explanation of the extent, if any, to which the child will not participate with nondisabled children in the regular class and in the activities described in subclause (IV)(cc);(VI)(aa) a statement of any individual appropriate accommodations that are necessary to measure the academic achievement and functional performance of the child on State and districtwide assessments consistent with section 612(a)(16)(A); and (bb) if the IEP Team determines that the child shall take an alternate assessment on a particular State or districtwide assessment of student achievement, a statement of why—AA) the child cannot participate in the regular assessment; and (BB) the particular alternate assessment selected is appropriate for the child; (VII) the projected date for the beginning of the services and modifications described in subclause(IV), and the anticipated frequency, location, and duration of those services and modifications; and (VIII) beginning not later than the first IEP to be in effect when the child is 16, and updated annually thereafter—(aa) appropriate measurable postsecondary goals based upon age appropriate transition assessments related to training, education, employment, and, where appropriate, independent living skills; (bb) the transition services (including courses of study) needed to assist the child in reaching those goals; and (cc) beginning not later than 1 year before the child reaches the age of majority under State law, a statement that the child has been informed of the child's rights under this title, if any, that will transfer to the child on reaching the age of majority under section 615(m). (ii) Rule of construction.—Nothing in this section shall be construed to require—(I) that additional information be included in a child's IEP beyond what is explicitly required in this section; and (II) the IEP Team to include information under 1 component of a child's IEP that is already contained under another component of such IEP." [http://idea.ed.gov/download/statute.html, Page 118 STAT. 2708]

If there is something instructive to be gleaned from the mind-numbing detail contained in the Individuals with Disabilities Education Act, it might be the need to articulate the rights that all children should have when it comes to an education. Some of those rights might include the following:

- an assessment of each student's present levels of performance and identifying at the earliest possible moment any learning difficulties that may affect academic performance (it might be argued some of this is already being done in the form of a report card);

- allow students, with their parents, to choose the school most ideally suited to their learning style;
- if a student is experiencing learning difficulties, a team will convene to develop a detailed plan specifying the interventional services to be provided, the frequency for such services, and a tracking mechanism to monitor progress;
- an explanation to the parents or guardians of the need for intervention, the type of supplemental support that child will receive, outcome goals and parental involvement requirements;
- alternative or modified assignments;
- specially designed instruction including delivery methods to assist the student's mastery of subject matter;
- in-classroom teacher's aides, and;
- access to any other related services that lead to effective learning progress.

The elements that most affect the long-term learning outcomes of a student include the involvement of parents, early learning, early intervention (applying remedial remedies as soon as a learning problem is recognized), and not promoting students to the next class or grade level when they clearly are incapable of meeting the prerequisites.

- **Parental involvement.** We must re-engage parents in the education of their children. Their involvement is needed from cradle through graduation. The biggest impact of parents, however, occurs in the child's earliest years, before pre-school. If we look at the Hart-Risley research study, *Meaningful Differences in the Everyday Experiences of Young American Children*, simply talking to children is critically important. This does not mean baby talk, and not military talk, as in, "do this, do that." What young children need is the kind of talk the Hart-Risley study refers to as "language dancing," real adult dialogue—full of open-ended questions, complex grammar and a rich vocabulary.

- **Early learning.** While parents and other caregivers can influence the development of cognitive thinking skills of infants, we need to start the more institutional form of our education system even earlier than kindergarten. Mandatory pre-school can establish the foundation to help prepare many more children for kindergarten and beyond. At age three, children can attend three half-day sessions per week. At age four, this can be increased to five half-day sessions.

- **Early intervention.** If teachers, principals, or other school personnel sense that a child is struggling with academic material, we must address the learning issue, head-on, at the earliest opportunity. Waiting to fix the learning difficulty is simply not an option. In order to have an effective system of early intervention, resources must be made available to teachers so the appropriate level of attention can be applied. Those resources can range from having access to a library of remedial material, online help in the form of mentors and tutors, on-site peer tutors, use of adaptive curricula, adult volunteers, and team teaching resources so that different teaching styles can be tried.

- **Stop passing on the problem.** In any case, we have to bring to a screeching stop the practice of grade promotion of students who have not acquired mastery of subject matter. Teachers must be empowered to determine which students have demonstrated competency. Those who have may move on to the next level. Those who have not may avail themselves of the interventions that are appropriate for their individual learning style and challenges.

The classroom. Teachers are clearly the most leveraged resource we have either to positively or negatively impact real classroom learning. A good teacher equals good educational outcomes. A bad teacher equals bad outcomes for children. Many people have commented that "insanely great teachers" simply does not scale up to system-wide reform. I agree there is a continuum of insane greatness. Achieving large-scale change will likely not happen without a culture of continuous improvement.

There are numerous benefits to applying a system of continuous improvement common in other industries, ranging from automobiles to hospitals, to personal improvement. There is no reason why continuous improvement cannot be applied to all aspects of the education system. Executed properly, the rewards of constant, continuous perseverance in improving the many facets of public school education are enormous.

Applied specifically to the most leveraged human capital (the teachers) in the public school education system, we must continually improve on the following areas:

- improve the quality of the students entering our colleges of education;
- implement new curricula for teachers that optimize teaching students in a "customized" way;
- increase the starting salaries for new teachers;
- offer bonuses to entice more teachers to pursue math and science, or to entice teachers to teach in the chronically tough schools;
- create an optional way to compensate teachers that is merit based, not set by rigid salary scales, and;

- if we are to move to a meritocracy in the teaching profession,
  we must have a better system for assessing teacher performance
  which includes both formative and summative evaluations.

We need to make good, solid hiring decisions and then continue
to develop a solid teaching corps...one teacher, one day at a
time. Incremental, lifelong professional improvement should
be the mindset in the teaching profession, as it is in, for example,
the practice of medicine. Continuous, ongoing professional
development should be the norm and not the exception
for teachers.

Attending workshops, seminars, conferences and other professional development venues should be crafted to the specific
developmental needs of each teacher in a way that results in
more effective teaching in the classroom. Team teaching where
feedback, advice and counsel from peers on different forms
of teaching, can be very helpful to both inexperienced and
experienced teachers. The really great teachers (that is, master
teachers) need to share their talents in ways that affect dozens
of other teachers and hundreds, if not thousands, of students.
Being committed to developing a solid corps of great teachers
also means we need to be constantly diligent in weeding out
those who simply are not cut out to be teachers.

No one should condone the arbitrary hiring or firing of any employee. A fair and comprehensive process is needed to review the performance of all public education employees who affect what happens in the classroom. The teacher assessment that is used at Lakeside School, a top-performing independent private school in Seattle, has been in place for eight years, and virtually all teachers at the school support it.

The evaluation criteria that Lakeside School employs takes account of what happens inside and outside of the classroom. Teachers are rated on whether they create a supportive learning environment for all students. Of the 26 specific criteria for evaluating what happens inside the classroom, perhaps the most impressive are the ones that assess how a teacher adjusts lessons to individual students. Consideration is given to the pace of learning and the level of difficulty of the material, as well as being able to adjust teaching strategies to match students' various listening styles and learning modes.

The eleven criteria used to assess teacher performance outside the classroom are equally comprehensive. They cover individual professional growth; communication skills and effectiveness with students, parents, colleagues and administration, and; support of the broader community that Lakeside School serves.

The Ohio Teacher Incentive Fund (OTIF) pioneered a teacher evaluation system that is more rigorous than the norm. Teachers are evaluated on the basis of multiple measures of performance, with frequent in-class observations conducted by experienced peer teachers. Monica Martinez, Vice President for Education Strategy at KnowledgeWorks, a non-profit entity that provides funding and leadership for education initiatives in Ohio, said:

> "An evaluation system that uses multiple measures and prioritizes the use of peer review, such as what has happened in Toledo, has tremendous potential to be one aspect of a larger professional development support system our teachers need. [from an article in Reuters Business & Finance, Jan. 29, 2008, *Two Ohio School Districts Cited for Strong Teacher Evaluation Models in New National Report on Promoting Teacher Quality. www.reuters.com/article/press Release*/idUS230506+20-Jan-2008+PRN20080129]

We must provide our teachers with the "human capital" tools that will allow them to create the student learning outcomes our society expects. One common theme that surfaced during my visits to classrooms and interviews with teachers and principals was a desire to have more adult help in the classroom. One principal commented, "Just having another adult present in the classroom changes the behavior of the students...and the teacher!" We really need to make available adult volunteers who can help with discipline, tutoring, mentoring on life skills, and moral support.

We should not try to centrally micromanage what happens in the classroom or the schools. The education system should give principals, teachers and their academic support team the authority to do what is best for their students. Top-down, centralized rules should be eased to allow principals and teachers the freedom to determine what curricula is best, how many days of teaching are necessary, the number of hours in the school day, how to assess the learning gains of students, the style of teaching, and any number of other issues best decided by those who are closest to the students.

The school. The vibrancy and success of a school will largely fall on the broad shoulders of the principal. In order to attract the best human capital, we must push more and more responsibility, decision making and resources for ensuring positive student outcomes to the school principal. This means implementing a number of important changes, ranging from establishing a set of metrics by which to measure goals, to unshackling principals from the web of centrally-imposed procedures and mandates, so they can innovate and make decisions that are appropriate for their schools.

This speaks directly to leadership. I believe great leaders like to "own" what they are responsible for. We should create an environment where they can lead and not simply administrate. We should give them real job satisfaction. Let them be the catalyst for constant and continual improvement at their school. Granting greater freedom to principals would lead to increased responsibility and accountability.

We need to provide the principal of each school with a capable Board of Directors or Trustees. These Trustees would be appointed by the governor or his surrogate. Their critical role would encompass the following: ensure that the right leadership is in place; and hire, evaluate, support and, if necessary, fire the principal.

These Trustees would be ultimately responsible for the school's direction and performance. Trustees would listen to their community to gain an appreciation for and an understanding of what their community expresses as key problems facing their school. Trustees would bring their unique gifts of experience, passion and leadership to help guide the principal and the school staff in developing a strategic plan and to oversee its operational implementation. Trustees would help provide long-term stability and assist with the development and preservation of the culture of the school.

The community. The resources of the broad community dwarfs even the most lavish public school budget. But we have to tap into it in strategic ways that can lead to real partnership and a synergistic environment.

There are many youth-serving agencies addressing a wide variety of social needs in our communities. Many groups have paid professional staff, proven programs, volunteers, and buildings that house their programs. I have often wondered why school facilities are not made more readily available to these youth-serving agencies. When the kids are in school, those facilities are fully utilized. When the kids aren't in school, those same facilities lie fallow (after school, weekends, breaks, holidays and summer vacation). The quid pro quo for using school facilities during non-academic times could be that the agency would provide professional staff to implement its youth programs on-site.

Boys & Girls Clubs and YMCAs, which invest heavily in facilities that are somewhat redundant to what schools already have (meeting space, multi-purpose rooms, gymnasiums), could avoid those capital needs. Rather than a model where the child goes to their facility, the child would simply stay at school after the closing bell rings to participate in any number of life skills, athletics or enrichment programs.

Girl Scouts and Boy Scouts have a long history of working with elementary schools in setting up scouting units that draw upon parents to serve as adult volunteer leaders. Troop meetings are typically held weekly, after school or in the early evenings, throughout the year. These are great programs that focus on developing life skills, building character, practicing leadership and establishing a strong foundation of values. They are not only effective, but they are also efficient. The overhead cost per child served is typically less than $15 per month.

While these aforementioned programs provide some mentoring and role modeling, even more extensive mentoring and tutoring resources can be brought in to help kids. These can be on-site or available through the internet. There are literally thousands of non-profit groups that dedicate themselves to helping kids. Each school's needs are different. So it should be up to each school's leadership team, led by the principal, to determine which non-profit groups are best for their school community, in order to achieve a specified outcome. Such outcomes might include reducing behavioral problems at the school, decreasing truancy, improving study habits, improving subject matter competency, or building a more involved parent community.

Corporate America also has a treasure chest of resources that it could apply to helping schools. Large companies have both financial assets and human capital. Many of them already support public education by giving to non-profit groups that work for school reform. Many are already sponsors of fundraising events which benefit these non-profits. But I think the most important asset corporate America has are its employees, past and present.

The potential impact of this army of well-educated professionals is enormous. Current employees, as well as company alumni, could be deployed in numerous ways. Senior executives can be appointed to the Board of Directors of local schools. Engineers and scientists could volunteer as math and science tutors in the classroom.

Information technology experts can help principals and teachers through the maze of technology options for improving the flow of information at local schools. Creative designers can lend a helping hand in art classes. Employees with a gift for a foreign language can be another voice for dialogue in any number of languages. Virtually everyone can help tutor young students, so all children are reading at grade level by grade four. The ways that employees can help is limited only by our imaginations and our will.

A few years ago, I helped found the Microsoft Alumni Foundation. Its creation was motivated by the desire to reconnect company alumni in ways that could make the world a better place. How many company alumni? Sixty thousand strong, and growing. This army of volunteers, with its shared Microsoft experience, can apply its talents and treasure to any number of issue initiatives, such as clean water, global warming, micro-lending, global health, ending poverty, women's rights, and even improving classroom outcomes in public schools.

There are many other corporate alumni organizations that can be formed for a similar purpose. Add to this, organizations like AARP (American Association of Retired Persons) with its almost one million members just in Washington state, and there is an abundant supply of volunteer resources.

CONCLUSION:
AN APPROACH TO PUBLIC
SCHOOL EDUCATION REFORM

*"There are always two choices. Two paths to take.
One is easy. And its only reward is that it's easy."*
UNKNOWN

The scope of what has to happen if we are to see real improvement in the learning outcomes for our kids in public schools is overwhelming. I have spent a considerable amount of time and energy getting up the learning curve on a subject that I did not know very much about one year ago. I have read numerous books and research papers, visited schools, met with teachers, principals, school superintendents, school board members, scholars, interested parents, business executives, foundation directors and politicians.

This book is the result of taking all the various inputs and articulating what I believe the problem is and then suggesting possible solutions. I reflect back to what I said in the Preface:

> "I believe the lack of sufficient emotional energy to make a
> positive difference in public education is due to the fact that
> we, as individuals, feel powerless to fix a problem that is a
> multi-headed hydra of gargantuan size."

So, how can we grapple with this monster? How can we approach the problem in a way that energizes all stakeholders?

The Japanese are largely credited with focusing on the benefits of long-term, continuous process improvement throughout all aspects of life. It all started with Toyota during the rebuilding of Japan after World War II. Kaizen (literally, "change to become good") is an original Japanese management concept for incremental, gradual and continuous improvement. Toyota Motors is world renowned for making Kaizen an integral part of its corporate culture. I believe the education industry would benefit greatly by applying Kaizen concepts.

Kaizen is a system that can involve everyone within the school district or school, as well as many external stakeholders. The beauty of Kaizen is that it does not rely on one big, audacious catalytic element for systemic change, or even on 11 planks of some book. Instead, it relies on the long-term view of encouraging everyone to participate in making small improvement suggestions, frequently and regularly.

Small, continuous improvement, applied assiduously by all stakeholders, can eventually lead to substantial change. Consideration should also be given to using Kaizen Blitz, a more concentrated form that focuses significant resources on a limited and narrowly defined objective.

CONCLUSION

Whether applying Kaizen, or Kaizen Blitz, perhaps a good place to start is to improve on the current mission statements for our public school systems. The mission statements of most public school systems are similar. Here is the mission statement for the Seattle Public Schools:

> "To provide every student with effective, high quality teaching and learning experiences, relevant curriculum and support services, in a safe and healthy environment."

Here is another:

> "Federal Way Public Schools is obligated to educate all students in academic knowledge, skills, abilities and responsible behavior to be successful, contributing members of a free society."

And, another:

> "The mission of the Tacoma Public Schools is to provide excellent instruction that results in increased student achievement and to create a dynamic partnership with parents and our community."

I think these mission statements are missing a few critical components. First, we need to make learning fun. Learning should be a constant adventure where young, malleable minds expand to explore history, relationships, and worlds that are of interest to each person Second, we need to make learning personal. Lastly, we need to arm each student with the feeling of being empowered to pursue his individual goals in life.

I offer the following supplement to the public school mission statement:

"Provide a joyful education that allows every child to pursue his dream."

It is my dream that this manifesto causes each of us to pause, take ten deep breaths, and imagine what needs to happen to reform our public school system of education. Surely, there will be many obstacles to overcome, numerous potholes to avoid, new paths to pave. We may not reach perfection. That's okay. As the French philosopher Voltaire said over two centuries ago, "The perfect is the enemy of good." Although these words are relevant today, we should also take care not to allow mediocrity to suffice for great!

Do we have the will, the courage and the perseverance to get the job done? The "we" represents hundreds of thousands, if not millions, of individuals. For "we" to have a voice will require action by individuals. Only you can answer this question. I can't answer it for you. But I can answer it for myself. My answer is a hopeful "YES!"

There is a Chinese proverb that says, "To get through the hardest journey we need take only one step at a time, but we must keep on stepping." Please join me on this journey by taking the next step. Go to www.outrageouslearning.org where we can further discuss the many issues of public school reform.

ABOUT THE AUTHOR

Scott Oki was born to Nisei parents who had been interned during World War II. His parents instilled a deep-rooted understanding of, and appreciation for the importance of a good education. They also made sure their first born son understood the meaning of hard work. He was picking strawberries, rasp-berries and beans at age 11 during summer "vacations." He also held jobs as a mailman, car wash attendant, percussion teacher, semi-professional musician, night service dispatcher, computer programmer, systems analyst, cost accountant and product mar-keting manager. He co-founded a software company in 1980.

In 1982, he joined a small software company in Bellevue, Washington, called Microsoft. He wrote a business plan and founded the International Division for the company. Four years later, the International Division accounted for 42 percent of the company's revenues and over 50 percent of Microsoft's world-wide profits. As the first Senior Vice President of the company, he then turned his attention to turning around Microsoft's money-losing U.S. Sales and Marketing Division. Three years later, the U.S. Sales and Marketing Division was producing over 20 percent of the operating profits of the company. Oki retired exactly ten years to the day of joining Microsoft.

Since his retirement in 1992, Oki has pursued his personal mission statement with a vengeance: "to marry my passion for things entrepreneurial with things philanthropic in ways that encourage others to do the same." He has been a full-time volunteer in the not-for-profit sector for over 16 years. Oki has served on close to 100 non-profit boards. He has founded or co-founded 15 non-profits, including Social Venture Partners, Densho, America's Foundation for Chess, Scoutreach Foundation, Executive Development Institute, Japanese American Chamber of Commerce, Microsoft Alumni Foundation, Seattle Police Foundation and SeeYourImpact.org.

Oki served for six years as a Regent for the University of Washington and as the President of the Board of Regents for one year. He was appointed by Governor Gary Locke to serve on the Governor's Commission on Early Learning.

He and his wife Laurie founded The Oki Foundation in 1987 and have given away millions of dollars, mostly to children's charities.

OUTRAGEOUS LEARNING
A DISCUSSION GUIDE

"Deliberation and debate is the way
to stir the soul of our democracy."
JESSE JACKSON, AMERICAN CIVIL RIGHTS LEADER

I n late 1986, when I inherited the money-losing U.S. Sales and Marketing Division for Microsoft, I undertook a painful, challenging, energy-draining and ultimately successful journey to turn the division around. It was truly transformative, involving new leadership, new processes, new values, new culture. Part of that new culture was the inclusive nature of involving key leadership in the active discussion of strategic issues. This manifested itself annually in something called "The Great Debates," a meeting of the division's senior executives and key managers.

Teams were assigned to research the issues. One team taking one side of the issue, the other team taking the opposite point of view. Each team selected a person to be the debater. The competitive nature of Microsoft led to some very creative and compelling arguments. In the end, we were all "winners". No one sacrificed his career because he had been assigned the unpopular side of an issue. There were substantial benefits derived from the debate process. The broad management team became educated on both sides of an issue. This had the direct effect that the team intimately understood the context in which key strategic decisions were made.

While I do not expect you to research issues affecting public school education reform, I do hope that the following questions can help you, and your friends and associates, to engage in lively discussion. This process of dialogue might actually lead to a groundswell of interest, action, policy change and, ultimately, better education outcomes for our children. This is perhaps the only way we can all be "winners."

QUESTIONS

1. Why change anything at all? My kids are doing just fine. They go to a great public school. They love their teachers. We make sure they do their homework. I don't want to risk changing the education they are currently getting for some unknown solution that will somehow make it better for everyone.

2. Shouldn't we have a standardized, national curriculum for K-12 education rather than allowing each school to decide what curricula is best for its students? The problem is so big. Isn't involvement at the federal level the only way to fix it?

3. Can you think of instances when you or your child had an insanely great teacher? What made the teacher insanely great?

4. Can you think of instances when you or your child had a not-so-great teacher? Did you notice any differences in how well you or your child learned new material? What were you able to do about the situation of a not-so-great teacher?

5. Do you want more freedom to choose the public school your child attends? Describe your priorities when identifying the qualities, attributes and traits of a school that would be an excellent choice for your child.

6. Who cares if school boards are elected or appointed? Isn't there just as much risk associated with electing or appointing an ineffective school board? What reasons can you think of to support an elected or an appointed school board?

7. Should school principals have discretion over more than five percent of school expenditures? How much discretion should they have? Why do you feel the way you do?

8. Do you think children should be held back a grade level when they are unable to show competence in subject matter? What interventions do you think should be available to help students who are not keeping pace with learning? By what means would you suggest that subject competency be measured?

9. Do you think teachers should be tenured? If not, how would you go about eliminating tenure? Do you think there should be a way to compensate teachers based on performance?

10. Do you know the annual salary ranges for public school teachers? On an annualized basis (180 days versus 240 days), do you think this compares favorably or unfavorably to other professionals? Do you think they are too little, too much or just right?

11. Should state teacher certification laws be abolished or changed? Why? What should change?

12. Parents are their children's primary teachers. Do you believe this statement? If so, why? If not, why not?

13. Should parents have a report card that accompanies their child's report card? What would a parent report card look like?

14. Only 70 percent of kids graduate from high school. There seems to be general agreement that this is not okay. What is an acceptable graduation rate?

15. Is it reasonable that all kids should be educated so they are qualified to go to college? What about the kids who simply do not want to go to college and would rather pursue a professional trade (as a chef, construction worker, draftsman, health care worker, etc.)? Should we allow them to pursue an alternative to a college-bound track?

16. Do you think the $9+ billion Washington state spends annually on K-12 education is spent effectively and efficiently? If you were Secretary of Education, what would you change?

17. If you could specify the skill set for the position of principal, what would it look like? Do you think a principal should be required to have a teaching certificate?

18. Private schools have Boards of Trustees. Do you think this is a good idea or bad idea for public schools? If public schools were to have Boards of Trustees, what do you think their role should be?

19. Should the school principal and his teaching team set the school calendar that is appropriate for their school? If this meant the school closest to your home went to a school calendar of 240 days per year, would this be okay with you? If there was a school located five miles away that had an 180-day school calendar, would you like to have the choice of sending your child there?

20. Should we make kindergarten attendance mandatory for all children? Should this state invest in mandatory preschool?

21. If you were in charge of our public schools and you could not increase the size of your budget, and you concluded the best way to improve learning outcomes would be to raise teacher salaries by 50 percent or to reduce class sizes by 25 percent, what other expenses would you cut?

22. There are 295 school districts in Washington State. Is this too few, too many, or just right? How do you think school districts should be organized?

23. Do you think teachers should have volunteer tutors and mentors available to help when students have difficulties? Would you be willing to help get your company to urge their employees to volunteer four hours per week in this capacity?

24. What is the role of the federal government in the public education system? Do you think the federal government role is appropriate? If not, what do you think is a more appropriate role and how would you go about influencing change?

25. When did you last express outrage over the state of the public school system? Was your voice heard? What do you think you can do to make sure your voice is heard?

26. If there is yet another attempt to get charter schools (not vouchers) approved in Washington state, would you support this effort? Why or why not?

27. How would you define a great education? What specific measures would you use?

28. Should the current system of grade levels be replaced with something else? What is that something else?

29. Is the money being spent by school districts on personal computers, software, maintenance contracts and information technology staff worth it? What tangible evidence is there to support your view?

30. How important do you think the education system is to the future of our country?

31. Only about half of the teachers who teach math and science actually have a degree in math or science. Is this okay? If not, what should be done about it?

32. There is research that shows social grade promotion is justi-fied because it damages the self esteem of the child to be held back a grade level. Do you think students should be promoted to the next grade level even though they have not demonstrated competency of the subject matter? Would you support social promotion if it were applied to your child?

33. Are your children getting a better or a worse education than you did? Can you identify some reasons why or why not?

34. Do you think a general breakdown in societal values and lack of discipline contributes to problems in the classroom? If so, what do you think should be done?

35. Early learning research shows that if a child is not reading at grade level by grade three, that child will likely never read at grade level. If this is true, and if a child cannot read at grade level by grade three, what should be done?

36. Should schools located in the most economically disadvan-taged neighborhoods receive extra funding? How much more funding? Would you attach any strings to this extra funding, or would you allow the school principal to deter-mine the best and most effective use of those funds?

37. Pretend for a moment that you won the Washington state lottery and you could start your own elementary school for 150 kids (without funding from the state). How would you go about doing this? Would you spend your money the same way that most school districts spend taxpayer money?

38. Which companies do you feel most effectively support public education reform? What specific programs that they support do you feel are working?

39. You have been appointed to the Board of Trustees for a public school which, based on any number of metrics, is not performing well (truancy rates are high, teacher turnover is high, discipline problems are getting worse, the PTA is almost non-existent). What would you do?

40. Who do you think should make teacher assignments? How much say should teachers have over where they teach? Do you think it is fair that the very best teachers can refuse assignment to a "difficult school," which could really use their experience, rather than assigning a newbie teacher who often fails in such a harsh indoctrination to teaching? Should a teacher receive higher pay to teach in a "difficult school"? Who should make this determination?

41. The Washington State Common School Manual for 2008 is about 1,500 pages (page numbers are not provided) of dense, eight-to-ten point type. As a practical matter, it is hardly ever used at the school level, let alone at the district level. Should the legislature review, simplify and re-write the hand-book? Should every statute affecting education have a sunset clause, so that it would force periodic review before renewal?

42. Obtain the current mission statement for your school or school district. Think about whether that statement adequately captures the essence of the education that occurs within the school or the school district. Re-write the mission statement for your school or school district.

43. Should public schools be based on a production line model or should they use a custom job shop model tailored to the individual needs of students?

44. What do you think about project-based learning?

45. What do you think about an interdisciplinary approach to teaching? What are the challenges of such an approach?

46. Do you think team teaching would work better than the more traditional model of one teacher per classroom?

47. Has technology in the classroom lived up to its promise? Can you point to specific examples of success or failure? Do you believe these examples are extensible to the general classroom, school, or school district?

48. How important is it to you that children are computer literate? Is this something that you feel schools should teach? If so, what does it mean to be computer literate?

49. How important is it to you that teachers are computer literate? What do you think happens in the classroom if a teacher is computer literate?

50. How long do you think it will take to reform public education?

51. Should a public education be a right or a privilege?

52. If you were the principal of a school, how much control would you want over what happens inside your school?

53. Do you think curricula specifically designed to incorporate the social networking phenomena should be developed?

54. What do you think is the most effective way to influence politicians and teachers unions regarding public school reform?

55. Do you think the Washington State Assessment of Student Learning (WASL) is a good way to measure the effectiveness of student learning? Should it be modified or replaced? How should it be modified? What should replace it?

56. Who should have the primary responsibility to develop great curricula? Private industry? Non-profit entities? Government? Teachers?

57. Is there a better way to reward teachers than the stereotypical method: years of experience and the earning of advanced degrees? What do you think are some characteristics of teaching that link directly to effectiveness?

58. How should schools of education change in order to produce better teachers?

59. Should we demand more accountability and involvement from parents, or should we simply assume little parental involvement and instead impose tougher discipline in the classroom?

ACKNOWLEDGMENTS

The first person I want to acknowledge is my wife Laurie. She convinced me to take on the task of trying to improve public education and then provided encouragement all along the way. Laurie was my harshest critic during the editing phase and although we agree to disagree on some of the issues, she has been wonderfully and lovingly supportive!

I am also grateful to the Washington Policy Center for wanting to work with and to publish an unpublished neophyte author like me. Thanks to Daniel Mead-Smith for the initial invitation to engage. Liv Finne saved me untold hours of research. Whenever I had a question, she was ready with an answer , the supporting data and the citation. Paul Guppy was my indispensible editor. I blame old age for having forgotten everything I learned about grammar and punctuation. I owe Paul a box of red leaded pencils!

The team at Girvin | Strategic Branding produced a beautiful vessel for my words. Tim Girvin...brilliantly creative. Virginia Sabado...maniacal attention to detail. Thank you for caring deeply about the look and feel of the book. It is beautiful.

There are so many others that I would like to thank for help-ing me during the writing of this book. You took time away from your own work to educate me on the various issues. You suggested other people to meet and publications to read. You were available to discuss and debate, on-line and off-line, day or night. You read the early, very rough drafts of the manuscript. You convinced me to take a breather when I was fraying at the edges. You reinforced that what we do and don't do to educate our kids will determine our fate. And, you didn't chuckle, laugh or guffaw when I said I was writing a book...on fixing public education.

Thank you all.

COLOPHON

This book was designed in collaboration with Scott Oki and the design team of Girvin, Seattle, located near the Pike Place Market. There are two typefaces used in the book, Girvalia—which is a classical, 1st-century, Roman stonecutting font for titling designed by Tim Girvin; and Dante, created by Giovanni Mardersteig in 1957, as a customized font for his small book press in Verona. The book is designed using the geometry of the golden section, based on medieval and renaissance theories of proportion and arrangement. The paper stocks are Cougar Opaque Vellum, the sleeve is Cougar Opaque Smooth and the debossed cover is a 4-color leather-bound patterning gathered from a 16th-century learning encyclopedia in the Girvin Rare Book Library.